Princess Diana
Lady of Fashion

Introduction by
Martina Shaw

Designed and produced by
Ted Smart and David Gibbon

GREENWICH HOUSE

Looking at early photographs of Lady Diana Spencer taken in her babyhood and when she was a leggy tomboy, it seems almost impossible to believe that, in such a short space of time, this little girl was to become the Princess of Wales – the most photographed woman in the world.

Perhaps those pictures of her when she first became front-page news are the most poignant. Rather than the trend-setter, she was then the trend follower, in her Sloane Ranger style clothes. The cashmere sweaters, sometimes worn over the shoulders and tied by the sleeves, and the casual skirts, bore the stamp of the Sloane Ranger. The brief glimpses seen of her hurrying between her flat and her car and the nursery school where she worked may have been responsible for her way of dressing being adopted in other countries, but it was already an established trend here.

It was really on the day that she became engaged to the Prince of Wales that Lady Diana Spencer became a leader of fashion. Copies of the magnificent sapphire and diamond engagement ring were very soon on sale for anything from a few pounds to a few thousand pounds, depending on whether they were made of coloured glass or the real thing. Of course the soft blue suit, which was the perfect foil for the engagement ring, was copied everywhere too, and the colour of the season became 'Lady Diana Blue.'

To compensate for the fact that she is rather tall, she took to wearing low heeled pumps. In a matter of weeks the shoe shops were full of 'Lady Di' shoes and many jobs have recently been saved in a Northern Ireland shoe factory, where they are working full time to keep up with the constant orders. Over a million pairs have been sold and they are still turning out a thousand pairs a week in the style inspired by the Princess of Wales.

The next sensation was the famous, strapless, black taffeta dress which Lady Diana wore at a gala performance which she attended with the Prince of Wales, just after they had become engaged. It seemed to be a very daring statement showing that, even though she was some years younger than Prince Charles, she was, none the less, a sophisticated young lady. On that occasion, they were accompanied by the elegant Princess Grace of Monaco, who was to die so tragically the following year. She seemed to be smiling encouragingly at the very young girl.

After that, whenever Lady Diana appeared in public she was photographed and every detail of every outfit was noted. Manufacturers all over the world rushed to try to be the first with a copy on the production line. The frilled necklines, which she frequently favours, were soon to become a feature on dresses and blouses in every fabric and every colour and in every price range.

She always chooses something appropriate for the occasion. In Wales she wore red and green, with a Celtic influence in style. In Scotland, of course, she wore tartan, with a stunning tam o' shanter. On each day of Royal Ascot people waited breathlessly to see what Lady Diana would be wearing. Every outfit was a winner and was complemented by a very becoming hat. There was a boater, a little shallow crowned hat tied with veiling, a feather trimmed tricorn – and people who had not been wearing hats in recent years saw how flattering they were and the milliners were in business again.

When the world was finally allowed to see the wedding dress, the details of which had been kept such a closely guarded secret, there were teams of workers, poised waiting to cut and sew and press and pack and have copies in the shop windows, in some cases, in a matter of hours later.

The dress, made of specially woven English silk, trimmed with antique lace, with its magnificent train of yards of lace-edged tulle, lightly scattered with tiny seed pearls and sequins, was of the proportions just right for the bride of the future King of England to wear in the great St Pauls Cathedral, but would certainly need to have been modified to have been worn in the village church!

The new Princess of Wales set off on her honeymoon in a striking outfit in azalea pink with a matching little tricorn hat, trimmed with ostrich plumes, and carrying a small clutch bag which immediately became a best seller among fashion accessories. The multi-strand choker pearl necklace, reminiscent of the Edwardian era, was also reproduced in every price range. The whole effect was chic without being too sophisticated, but the Princess of Wales has style, even when she is standing knee deep in a lake wearing waders.

How blessed we are that our young ambassadress of fashion is such a natural beauty. Who better to show off the clothes which we are capable of producing in this country than this tall slender girl with her classic good looks.

No doubt there will be many occasions when she will visit foreign countries with her husband and the eyes of the world will be on them. Let us hope that our designers and couturiers will make the most of such golden opportunities. In doing so, they will also be helping the whole fashion industry in this country and many of its satellite industries.

Martina Shaw

Clothes for all seasons; clothes for all reasons
selection of Diana's wide range of outfits, wor
since her first official outing as prospective br
to the Prince of Wales, and contributing to a
constantly changing and extended wardrobe
suit every occasion. Highlights of her varied
personal and public life comprise the group
above – (left to right) that famous black silk
taffeta dress which, with its plunging necklin
launched David and Elizabeth Emanuel almc
spectacularly as it launched Diana herself; th
stunning bright red coat and veiled hat (seen
right) which Diana wore at a carol concert at
Guildford Cathedral in December 1981; the
summery heavy-spotted flame-red dress and
large hat with the fly-away brim for the Lond
wedding in May 1981 of Nicholas Soames; a
heavy, warm and brightly-coloured coat in W
wool for the luncheon at London's Guildhall
following the announcement of her pregnanc
November; and the maternity dress in which
first appeared outside St Mary's Hospital,
Paddington after her baby was born. Those
loose-fitting dresses, usually in soft colours, w
a natural and continuing feature of her much-
publicised pregnancy: they included the pale
smock worn in February (left) on her return f
a ten-day holiday in the Bahamas, and a pale
pink dress for her last public outing at Smith's
Lawn, Windsor in June (far left).

Diana can look good in almost anything. The Emanuels' classic, unforgettable wedding gown was a triumph with its unashamedly ornate frills, bows and ruffles, its panels of sequin-studded lace and that billowing train. Its Victorian extravagance exactly suited Diana's tall, graceful figure and despite those creases in the silk puff-ball skirt, the first public sighting of it almost took the breath away. Three weeks later (above) the splendour of the wedding gave way to the easy informality of a camera-call at Balmoral. Diana matched Prince Charles' casual country garb with a loose-fitting dog-toothed jacket and skirt, the closest she came to Scottish plaid until the Braemar Games the following month. In June 1982 (left) she emerged from hospital with Prince William, wearing an ordinary green polka-dot pre-natal dress.

The distinction between the formal, semi-formal and informal, and between privacy and publicity, is often a fine one. A light, filmy dress with a crisp flower print (top left) was chosen for Diana's three-hour visit with Prince Charles to Gibraltar, *en route* for a two-week honeymoon cruise in the Mediterranean, but a simple, blush-pink wrap-over dress (above) suited her meeting, at the end of that luxurious fortnight,

with Madame Sadat in Egypt.
A practical black coat (left) kept out stiff breezes around the Scilly Isles in April 1982, while the bright pink coat Diana wore at the beginning of Queen Beatrix's four day State Visit to London the following November added just the right degree of dash to a formal occasion (opposite).

11

The same smiling good humour characterised two of Diana's most recent engagements, but there was a striking contrast in her headgear. She sported a typical John Boyd creation (far left and opposite page) for her visit in mid-December 1982 to University College Hospital in London. It followed the small cap formula which the Princess has favoured with great regularity, but in this case its petite, close-fitting design was spectacularly set-off by an almost unruly burst of ostrich feathers, which immediately tended to take the eye away from the veil – another feature which is also fast becoming a Diana hallmark. The pure white colour of the feathers illuminated the otherwise sombre, wintry character of her outfit that day. Something a little lighter, yet equally classy (above, left and below), for her return to Wales at the end of November: the generously-proportioned beret with its warm, light brown tones, performed the dual function of topping out a stylish coat which, incidentally, reached almost down to Diana's ankles, covering so much of the back of her head that it success-fully allowed the whole of her face to be seen by an admiring public – a consideration which all female members of the Royal Family must take into account when choosing additions to their collections of millinery.

A couple of popular repeat performances. In October 1982 Diana – a picture of health despite growing rumours about anorexia nervosa – breezed into Cardiff's New Theatre for a performance by the Welsh National Opera (this page) wearing a flowing, pale blue chiffon dress with its wide sequinned sash. She had worn the same evening gown for the State banquet given by the King of Saudi-Arabia at Claridges in London in June 1981. (Opposite) the Bellville-Sassoon dress that entranced everyone at the *Splendour of the Gonzaga* exhibition in London in November 1981 was worn again a year later for the première of *Gandhi* at the Odeon Cinema, Leicester Square. Here, the flood of soft pink, blue and lilac and the fineness of the silk chiffon fabric were beautifully complemented by the colourful tones of Diana's bouquet.

This is probably the most entrancing evening dress Diana has worn to date. Designed by Bellville-Sassoon, its blend of the softest colours enhance the femininity of the unabashed off-the-shoulder neckline, and the delicacy of the filmy silk chiffon material. Reckoned to be one of her favourites, the dress was worn for Diana's attendance at the London première of *Gandhi* in December 1982. A year earlier she wore it to the *Gonzaga* exhibition in London, though with one of her ornate pearl chokers instead of this heavy pendant with the Prince of Wales feathers design.

Another favourite – though in the day-coat department and strictly confined to the winter of 1981/2 – was the smart, loose fitting coat which Diana is seen wearing (right) at a fair organised by children and staff at a Brixton school in January 1982. Worn also for the previous Christmas Day's service at St George's Chapel, Windsor, the absence of a belt heralded the onset of maternity at a time when Diana was almost four months pregnant. The warm turquoise was perfect for a dismally wintry month, and the heavy motifs on the collar added a touch of Spring. There was similar emphasis on stitching and seaming around the shoulders when Diana visited a youth aid centre in South London in November 1982 (below) and all three occasions pictured on these pages evidence her love of slightly puffed sleeves where the coat material is gathered at the shoulder. (Opposite) the gathering gives a wide-shouldered illusion to this blonde-brown cashmere coat, worn long and loose for a visit to the Elephant and Castle in December 1982.

After the romantic magnificence of her wedding and a honeymoon which seemed, as one newspaper reader complained, "to go on for ever," anticipation of Diana's handling of her first public engagement as Princess of Wales mounted. Much of this was attributable to the novelty of seeing her and Prince Charles on duty together as man and wife for the first time, but there was no small interest in forecasting the cut of Diana's autumn clothes. In the result, her choice was everywhere acclaimed, and for John Boyd, of Brompton Arcade, her most favoured

milliner, the sounds of congratulation must have been sweet. His creations triumphed on the second and third day of the tour of Wales, when Diana wore each of two styles of his range of close-fitting headgear. On 28th October (top left) the brimless hat in soft beige was beautified by a generous veil and a huge plume of ostrich feathers which were animated by strongish winds. With it, Diana sported the warm, long-lapelled, loosely tied light brown cashmere wrap coat which emphasised her slimmer figure, and the white pie-frill blouse which by then had become an almost indispensable part of her wardrobe. It was very much a toss-up which outfit was the better – that one, or the deep aubergine ensemble she wore the following day in South Wales (above, far left and opposite page). Here again was John Boyd's small hat, but its perky brim and the almost enveloping plunging feather gave it a romantic, swashbuckling look, relieving the comparative plainness of the rich velvet jacket with its matching gathered skirt. Again, the ruffed blouse is prominent, offering a sharp contrast to the muted tone of the outfit as a whole, for even the ornamentation on the jacket was kept to a minimum of unobtrusive scrolled embroidery down the front panels. Diana is one of the few royal ladies who can happily dispense with a hat even on official occasions: as the photograph (left) on previous pages show, her own hair-style, modified as it gradually has been over the months, has become a symbol of her appeal to the fashionable aspirations of the young.

Diana has acquired a reputation for being prey
to uncertainties and fits of sullenness, though all
too often on the evidence of a chance
photograph showing her pensively off-guard.
She does seem to suffer from a tendency to be
overwhelmed by extreme formality, and by the
same token, has always been at her very best in
circumstances which give her the opportunity to
shine in her own natural, approachable way.
Certainly she appeared a little unsure of herself
(top) on her first visit to Cheltenham in March
1981, and again as recently as November 1982
(top right), when attending Queen Beatrix's
State banquet at Hampton Court Palace – and
this despite her dazzling dress and glittering
jewellery. But there were unrelieved smiles as,
suntanned and patently very much in love, she
posed with Prince Charles for photographs at
the Brig o' Dee near Balmoral in August 1981
(top centre and far right) and the look of
confidence increased as the Welsh tour got
underway two months later (above and opposite
page). Even the photographer got his picture
(right) without incurring instant disapproval!

An early example of Diana's crisp, bright ideas came when, with Prince Charles, she visited Tetbury (below) in May 1981. It was very much a trip to meet her future neighbours, because Tetbury is the nearest town to Highgrove House, the Wales' Gloucestershire country retreat. The eye-catching snow-storm pattern on a brilliant red jacket was complemented,

again, by that white frilled blouse and the whole even outshone the masses of flowers she carried with her. On formal evening occasions, necklines continued to plunge, though not quite as daringly as at Goldsmiths Hall in March 1981 (inset right) when her revealing black taffeta dress caused such a sensation that she has never publicly been seen in it again. Perhaps the most stunning follow-up was the deep sapphire blue velvet evening dress (right) she wore to a dinner at 11 Downing Street in February 1982: designed by Bellville Sassoon it was perfectly matched by her sapphire engagement ring and handsome drop earrings, and the lavish lace-trimmed necklace made it an aristocrat among her wardrobe of evening gowns. A more modest version was seen the following month when Diana and her husband attended a variety performance at the Barbican Centre (opposite page, main picture): the dress suggested rubies rather than sapphires, but diamond and pearl jewellery provided the sparkle, and the square neck bore only a fraction of the embellishment of its earlier counterpart. For sheer elegance, the superb floaty dress Diana chose for her November 1981 evening visit to the Victoria and Albert Museum was unbeatable, its rippling, flounced yoke and a gorgeous stranded choker emphasising the unusual expanse of bare shoulder.

Any survey of Diana's clothes will show
that – to put it nicely – she is no slave to
fashion or – to put it more bluntly – she
has not always attracted widespread
approval of her choice. The strange,
though admittedly striking combination
(above) of the weightless, billowing blue
dress and the heavy, rather hairy red coat
presumably owed more to practicality –
she was six months pregnant and Aintree
in April can be chilly – than to good
fashion sense. But the white-spotted
black dress beneath another weighty
deep pink coat which she had worn at
Huddersfield the previous month
(opposite page bottom left) presented
another example of an odd twinning of
clothes. She was not even looking her
best on her return to London (opposite
page bottom right) from carrying out
engagements in Leeds, wearing a dark
green coat – again rather too heavy even
for her statuesque figure – with large
black Victorian gothic motifs on the front
panels. These few examples contrast
badly with the pleasant, airy outfit she
chose for her last official engagement, at
Deptford, before the birth of Prince
William. This bright blue polka-dot
maternity dress (opposite page top left)
highlighted by a three-strand pearl
choker and the smartest of hair-dos was
just the right choice for a warm, late
spring day. A year earlier she sported this
soft pink leaf design dress (opposite page
centre) as a casual alternative to her
"official" clothes: here she watched
Prince Charles at polo. Later in 1981,
more formal occasions called forth more
formal clothes. The colourful plaid she
had worn at the September Braemar
Games came out again for the ceremonial
planting of commemorative saplings in
Hyde Park that November (opposite page
top right) while an all enveloping black
cape (right) covered the bright green
chiffon evening dress chosen for a gala in
Swansea the previous month.

The blue polka-dot dress Diana wore at Deptford had already had one airing – on the first day of her visit to the Scilly Isles with Prince Charles in April 1982 (opposite page and above right), though she then preferred a necklace to a choker. Another maternity dress – the bright pink one (far right) was only worn once in public, at a Windsor polo match early in June. Other one-off outfits included (curiously) the glowing red coat and hat worn at Guildford in December 1981 (top), the warm pink combination – her smart pillbox was replaced for a time by a protective helmet – chosen for her visit to the Sony factory at Bridgend in April 1982 and, less surprisingly, the red and green tribute to the Welsh (above) which sensationalised her first official visit to Wales in October 1981. Pink became a favourite in autumn 1982 (right) and the ruffed neckline remained so.

It is a measure of Diana's dress sense that not only does she know when to avoid flamboyance, but also that on such occasions she can still look chic without looking beyond her years. The Falklands service at St Paul's in July 1982 illustrated this – a fairly demure blue dress respected the sombre undertones of the occasion (above and right), while the overwhelming black dictated by royal mourning for the Princess Grace of Monaco the following September (top centre, top right) merely emphasised her smooth English-rose complexion. Black, too, for remembrance – the same coat (top left) graced the Festival of Remembrance at the Albert Hall in November, though with the addition of large poppies on, unusually, the right side. (Opposite page) Diana leaving the Wellington Barracks the following day after the service of Remembrance there.

(Opposite) classic good looks enhanced by unquestionable style: Diana in good form with the Welsh crowds during her visit to Aberdyfi and Barmouth at the end of November 1982. An almost maxi-length light brown coat was relieved by wide-squared lines in black, and these echoed the uncompromising black trim, buttons and gloves. Knee-length boots completed the accessories and a large, rakishly-slung suede beret, trimmed with a darker brown matched with her handbag, completed a fine effect. Her sweep of long fair hair and winning smile make this an excellent study of a popular princess. (Right) a similar colour scheme for her visit to Capital Radio in London two days earlier: her coat, lighter in weight and colour, is trimmed at the collar, while its pallor is reflected in the milky neck-scarf. Diana willingly weathered the risks of not wearing a hat, although the wind had already begun to dishevel her hairstyle.

Although Diana tends to favour pinks and reds, she has occasionally experimented with green. (Above) one of the earlier attempts which, in Leeds in March 1982, did not come off as well as the lush green velvet suit with its matching hat (above left) worn for a visit to the Royal School for the Blind at Leatherhead the following November. (Top) stark white collars brightened dullish bottle green plaid, and enabled Diana to accede gracefully to the demands of Scottish tradition at the Braemar Games in September 1982. Something of a contrast (left) as Diana tried out a grey coat with collars and cuffs picked out in black, and a smart red band to her matching black tam-o'-shanter.

Diana's flair for beautiful clothes is now beginning to be matched by her liking for sparkling jewellery. Positive assistance has come from the Queen herself, who lent her delicate diamond necklace to Diana for her visit to Barbican in March 1982 (left), but the high choker comprising no fewer than six strands of pearls and a diamond clasp – as worn for the *Gonzaga* exhibition in November 1981 (below far left) – is her own. So too is the much less conspicuous emerald choker she wore to the première of *E.T.* in London's Leicester Square in December 1982 (opposite page). Compare this with the conspicuous lack of jewellery on other occasions – earrings only, for her trip to Yorkshire in March 1982 (far left) and for her first solo engagement in November 1981 (below), and just a couple of bracelets to complement the glitter of her electric-blue evening dress as she left a London cinema after watching the James Bond film *For Your Eyes Only* in March 1981.

The slinky, blue silk dress in which Diana arrived (opposite page) at a charity fashion show at London's Guildhall in November 1982 signified a departure in her own tastes as well as from the almost standard ball-gown format. Its essentially 'thirties style avoided wide skirts in favour of a dropped waist, preferred the novel one-shoulder neckline to the usual symmetrical plunge, and put its designer Bruce Oldfield firmly on the map. With her three-strand pearl choker and matching bracelet, this very feminine creation not only outshone many of the show's exhibits, but maintained Diana as a fashion innovator. Compare the more classic style of the dress worn (left) at Cardiff the previous month.

The Emanuel's deep blue velvet dress – one of the most grandiose Diana wore in 1982 – was twice worn that year. The difference was in the necklace: in February Diana favoured a simple pearl rope with a small sapphire pendant; in December she attended a charity concert at the Festival Hall in London (above and top right) setting off the gown with a massive sapphire pendant on a gold chain – part of the fabulous £3/4 million wedding gift from the Saudi-Arabian Royal Family. (Above right) a third showing for the emerald green silk taffeta gown at the Barbican in October – it achieved fame as the first evening dress she was officially photographed in. Among Diana's recently-acquired day clothes are the simple pink suit she first wore at London's Hospital for Sick Children in December (right); the somewhat more ornate creation worn first at a private wedding, and then (far right) for the arrival of the Dutch Royals in November, and the no-nonsense red coat with its black collar – now a favourite stylistic flourish – in which she visited children at a South London adventure playground in December.

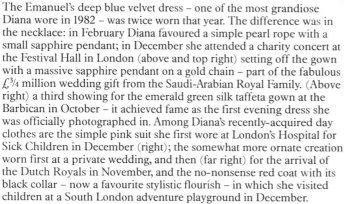

The dress that launched a volley of criticisms was the shocking-pink two-piece Diana wore early in September 1982 at the wedding of her former flat mate, Carolyn Pride (left and opposite page). Windy weather unfortunately emphasised the overall shapelessness of the suit, with its baggy, low waist, long ribbons dangling from the sailor-suit collars, and the hat which seemed out of all proportion to the outfit as a whole. Foremost critic was Hollywood designer Richard Blackwell who compared her to "a 1910 bathing beauty from a Mack Sennet silent movie." He might well have been thinking of that day at Aintree (above) when he also accused her of going off "into Queen Victoria's attic" and "looking so unlike the marvellous progressive girl she once was." All of which explained why he placed Diana among 1982's Ten Worst Dressed Women. Voted one of the most elegant in 1981, she will presumably not have taken the criticism too seriously. She probably echoes Prince Charles' sentiments – that when you can be voted best *and* worst dressed within twelve months, ignore it all and opt for personal comfort.

One of Diana's few official engagements in April 1982 involved a visit to Liverpool to open a Chinese Community Centre. For it, she chose a colourful deep-pink ensemble consisting of fundamentally simple lines enlivened by bows and frill. Her coat, for instance, betrayed her weakness for the wide-shouldered look with its copious yoke, and incorporated the neck-frill which normally emanates from a blouse. An unusual addition to a plain but pretty hat was the large velvet bow tacked beneath its medium-sized brim.

A paler pink ensemble was chosen for Diana's trip to Bridgend shortly after the Liverpool visit (left and bottom). The mandarin-collared coat is unadorned but her small pillbox hat sported an attractive large petal ornament. Pink shades set off her complexion as effectively as the soft honey colour worn at Capital Radio in November 1982 (bottom far left) matched her light hair. In evening wear she is equally at home in light or dark coloured creations: (below) her pale, soft coloured gown has an almost translucent quality while (opposite page and far left) her white and champagne coloured dress sparkled with silver flashes. Examples of Diana's choice of darker colours include the deep salmon-pink and gold evening dress – with that black cloak again – for an Albert Hall concert in March 1982 (below left) and the unusually sombre red, purple and black for the *E.T.* première in December (bottom left).

More evidence of Diana's predeliction for pink came in November and December 1982. Prettiest was her suit (right and above right) for the welcoming ceremonies for Queen Beatrix of the Netherlands' arrival in London on a sharp November morning. The outfit glowed with the warmth of its colour and looked as if it was keeping its wearer warm too. At the same time its fabric-covered buttons, large rich floral pattern and luxurious integral ruffle round the neck were sufficiently feminine to obviate the need for heavy jewellery – unobtrusive pearl-drop earrings and the merest glimpse of her pearl choker were sufficient. A fortnight later she delighted staff and patients at the Great Ormond Street Hospital for Sick Children in London with another warm-coloured suit, this time in a crushed raspberry shade (above) for which the extruding frill of a white silk blouse provided one highlight, while the soft pinks and whites of her official bouquet provided another. It is said that details of floral presentations are given in advance in order to facilitate the right choice of royal clothes. There was a graduation to red four days later when Diana wore a handsome woollen dress in a rich burgundy tone for a visit to a playgroup in Wandsworth (top and far right). Again, a sweeping yoke and ruched sleeves gave her shoulders the additional width which her tallish figure can readily accommodate, and a line of fabric-covered buttons complemented the effect of the gatherings. (Opposite) a symphony in emerald green.

For Diana the hat has not yet become *de rigueur* and she picks and chooses the occasions for which one might be suitable or desirable. On the whole, she seems to prefer to be without one. The hat she wore at

Leeds in March 1982 was discarded for the journey back to London (top centre). Nor did she wear one for the outdoor ceremony in November 1981 when she switched on the Christmas illuminations in Regent Street (above), nor for her return from holiday in the Bahamas the following February (top), an official visit to Huddersfield in March (right), or to Deptford in May (far right). Two examples of the perfect compromise were provided by headgear in Scotland in September 1982 (opposite) and in Wales two months later (top right).

Something completely different for Diana as she paid a short visit to the Royal Marsden Cancer Centre in London in mid-December 1982. Here was an unusually striking outfit which comprised a two-piece busy pattern with large, colourful, shield-like formal motifs, and incorporating a neat bolero over the sharp, shining turquoise of her silk blouse. A large expanse of matching scarf adorned the neck, offering a pleasantly informal alternative to her usual frills, while black shoes and accessories, and the faintest white sheen of her tights completed the impression of a very polished, womanly appearance. (Opposite) the simpler suited style, also in London the previous week.

e remaining photographs on these
ges show Diana in clothes worn for the
st time in public in autumn 1982,
esumably from the extensive wardrobe
 outfits purchased the previous summer.
here was a minor scandal when, in
ctober, it was rumoured that in a fit of
que, born of boredom on holiday at
lmoral, she suddenly travelled down to
ndon to spend a fortune on a whole
nge of garments. If the story is true, it
ys a lot for the power of a tantrum to
fluence the choice of suitable and
tractive clothes. She certainly looked
ppy enough, whether on strictly formal
casions in Wales (top left) or on more
surely assignments with young children
 South London (opposite page, top).

Few pictures, official or otherwise, have illustrated the progress of Prince William in his early months. That is something of a disappointment to millions of royal-watchers, but is explained by Diana's desire not to expose her son to over-zealous publicity. The main occasions on which William has been seen, however, have illustrated a wide range of his mother's preferences in clothes. The very informal exit from hospital (below left) on 22nd June 1982 was characterised by the well-worn maternity dress she slipped on for the journey back to Kensington Palace. Nothing could have contrasted more explicitly with Diana's regal, composed attitude as portrayed by Lord Snowdon in a fine study to commemorate her twenty-first birthday in July (left). Taken some weeks before Prince William's birth, the photograph shows Diana wearing a splendid Victorian-style blouse, lace-yoked and high-necked, its wealth of intricate patterns projecting the smoothness of her complexion. The Queen Mother's 82nd birthday that August was honoured by Prince William's christening at Buckingham Palace, and Diana wore a mature cyclamen-coloured dress with a busy pattern of ox-eye daisy petals and a sweeping, wide-brimmed pink hat with matching fabric band (below right). The low square-cut neckline was not one of Diana's customary favourites, but the high, frilly blouse was back again – and with frilly cuffs to match – just before Christmas for some delightfully informal photographs of William at precisely six months of age (top left, below and opposite page). Diana may have been a trifle overdressed for this cosy, domestic photo-call, but she is never one to miss the opportunity to look well.

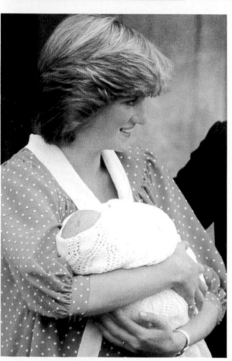

There was an air not so much of contentment as of elation as, for first time, Diana posed with her three-week-old son (left) Prince William Arthur Philip Louis, for official pictures which the world eager to see and to publish. As for most significant commemorati occasions in the Princess' recent life, Lord Snowdon was assigned the task of portraying the important bond between mother and ch which psychologists insist can never be too highly accentuated, a few people disagreed that he excelled in its execution. This photograph was one of several released on 29th July 1982 to mark Charles' and Diana's first wedding anniversary, and the proud fath made up the trio (bottom centre) as a willing recruit to the novel experience of fatherhood. Diana's silky, deep-cream dress with its irregular, self-spot pattern lending an additional sheen, was pleas casual, reflecting her husband's choice of open-necked shirt to ad touch of informal domesticity to the studies. Her gold and pearl necklace with the heart-shaped pendant afforded a simple but ap complement to the dress' overall colour. Two other pictures evide Diana's complete informality on essentially private occasions, no matter how historically significant: (bottom right) heavily pregna but enjoying the fun at a polo match at Smith's Lawn, Windsor ea in June 1982, and (below left) wearing exactly the same, now voluminous-looking, dress as she and Prince Charles emerged fro Mary's Hospital Paddington three weeks later with Britain's future king in the arms of his father. (Opposite page) a well-groomed Di at the start of her visit to the Charlie Chaplin Adventure Playgrou South London in December 1982: half an hour later her hair was windswept as she accompanied a young boy through the playgrou

58

"A gallery of royal smiles" might well describe this selection of photographs some of Diana's many engagements in 1982. (Opposite) wide-eyed interest in the goings on at the January fair of the Dick Sheppard Mixed Comprehensive School at Tulse Hill, where the proceeds of the event helped to send children on an educational trip to Zimbabwe. (Bottom left) a happy visit to the Lewis Lane playgroup in Cirencester in November, where Diana stayed twice as long as planned, reading stories to toddlers and helping them with their games and other activities. (Top centre) coats off four days later in Wrexham, where she promised to bring Prince William as soon as she could. (Above) a cheerful reception at the South London Advice Centre in Lewisham, where Diana learned the problems of mothers who were either unemployed or on low wages, running one-parent families. The visit to the centre, which helps some three thousand youngsters a year, took place on 30th November. (Far left) another noisy welcome from hundreds of nurses and onlookers as Diana arrived at the Great Ormond Street Hospital for Sick Children early in December: as expected, she was at her very best exchanging banter with young patients. (Top left) Diana in more pensive mood as she ran the gauntlet of strikers on picket duty during her visit the following day to the Department of Health and Social Security headquarters in South London. (Above left) Diana leaving the Royal Marsden Centre on 1 December, complete with gift for Prince William.

First English edition published by Colour Library Books
© 1983 Illustrations and Text: Colour Library International Ltd.
   99 Park Avenue, New York, N.Y. 10016, U.S.A.
This edition published by Greenwich House, a division of Arlington
House, Inc., distributed by Crown Publishers, Inc.
h g d e d c b a
Colour separations by REPROCOLOR LLOVET, Barcelona, Spain.
Display and text filmsetting by ACESETTERS LTD., Richmond, Surrey, England.
Printed and bound in Barcelona, Spain by JISA-RIEUSSET and EUROBINDER.
All rights reserved
ISBN 0-517-414-902

CRESCENT 1983

D. L. B.: 5.814